My Most Beautiful Dream

Min aller fineste drøm

A picture book in two languages

Audiobook and video:

www.sefa-bilingual.com/bonus

Password for free access:

English: **BDEN1423**

Norwegian: **BDNO2324**

Cornelia Haas · Ulrich Renz

My Most Beautiful Dream

Min aller fineste drøm

Bilingual children's picture book,

with audiobook for download

Translation:

Sefâ Jesse Konuk Agnew (English)

Werner Skalla, Jan Blomli, Petter Haaland Bergli (Norwegian)

Lulu can't fall asleep. Everyone else is dreaming already – the shark, the elephant, the little mouse, the dragon, the kangaroo, the knight, the monkey, the pilot. And the lion cub. Even the bear has trouble keeping his eyes open ...

Hey bear, will you take me along into your dream?

Lulu får ikke sove. Alle andre drømmer allerede – haien, elefanten, den lille musa, dragen, kenguruen, ridderen, apen, piloten. Og løveungen. Til og med bamsen kan nesten ikke holde øynene åpne ...

Du bamse, kan du ta meg med inn i drømmen din?

And with that, Lulu finds herself in bear dreamland. The bear catches fish in Lake Tagayumi. And Lulu wonders, who could be living up there in the trees?

When the dream is over, Lulu wants to go on another adventure. Come along, let's visit the shark! What could he be dreaming?

Og med det er Lulu allerede i bamsenes drømmeland. Bamsen fanger fisk i
Tagayumisjøen. Og Lulu lurer på hvem som bor der oppe i trærne?
Når drømmen er over, vil Lulu oppleve enda mer. Bli med, vi skal hilse på
haien! Hva drømmer han om?

The shark plays tag with the fish. Finally he's got some friends! Nobody's afraid of his sharp teeth.

When the dream is over, Lulu wants to go on another adventure. Come along, let's visit the elephant! What could he be dreaming?

Haien leker sisten med fiskene. Endelig har han venner! Ingen er redde for de spisse tennene hans.

Når drømmen er over, vil Lulu oppleve enda mer. Bli med, vi skal hilse på elefanten! Hva drømmer han om?

The elephant is as light as a feather and can fly! He's about to land on the celestial meadow.

When the dream is over, Lulu wants to go on another adventure. Come along, let's visit the little mouse! What could she be dreaming?

Elefanten er lett som en fjær og kan fly! Snart lander han på skyene.
Når drømmen er over, vil Lulu oppleve enda mer. Bli med, vi skal hilse på
den lille musa! Hva drømmer hun om?

The little mouse watches the fair. She likes the roller coaster best.
When the dream is over, Lulu wants to go on another adventure. Come
along, let's visit the dragon! What could she be dreaming?

Den lille musa ser seg om på tivoli. Hun liker best berg- og dalbanen.

Når drømmen er over, vil Lulu oppleve enda mer. Bli med, vi skal hilse på dragen! Hva drømmer han om?

The dragon is thirsty from spitting fire. She'd like to drink up the whole lemonade lake.

When the dream is over, Lulu wants to go on another adventure. Come along, let's visit the kangaroo! What could she be dreaming?

Dragen er tørst etter å ha sprutet ild. Helst vil han drikke opp hele sjøen med brus.

Når drømmen er over, vil Lulu oppleve enda mer. Bli med, vi skal hilse på kenguruen! Hva drømmer han om?

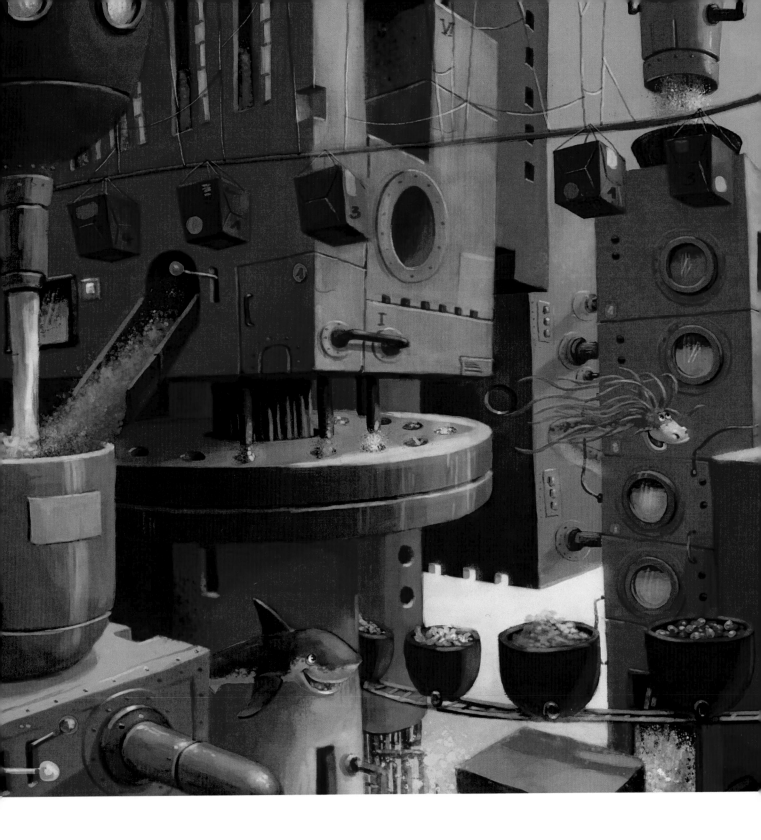

The kangaroo jumps around the candy factory and fills her pouch. Even more of the blue sweets! And more lollipops! And chocolate!

When the dream is over, Lulu wants to go on another adventure. Come along, let's visit the knight! What could he be dreaming?

Kenguruen hopper gjennom godterifabrikken og stapper pungen sin full.
Enda flere av de blå dropsene! Og enda flere kjærlighet på pinne! Og
sjokolade!

Når drømmen er over, vil Lulu oppleve enda mer. Bli med, vi skal hilse på
ridderen! Hva drømmer han om?

The knight is having a cake fight with his dream princess. Oops! The whipped cream cake has gone the wrong way!

When the dream is over, Lulu wants to go on another adventure. Come along, let's visit the monkey! What could he be dreaming?

Ridderen er i kakekrig mot drømmeprinsessen sin. Oi! Kremkaken bommer!

Når drømmen er over, vil Lulu oppleve enda mer. Bli med, vi skal hilse på apen! Hva drømmer han om?

Snow has finally fallen in Monkeyland. The whole barrel of monkeys is beside itself and getting up to monkey business.

When the dream is over, Lulu wants to go on another adventure. Come along, let's visit the pilot! In which dream could he have landed?

Endelig har snøen kommet til apelandet! Hele apegjengen er ute og gjør apestreker.

Når drømmen er over, vil Lulu oppleve enda mer. Bli med, vi skal hilse på piloten! I hvilken drøm har han landet?

The pilot flies on and on. To the ends of the earth, and even farther, right on up to the stars. No other pilot has ever managed that.

When the dream is over, everybody is very tired and doesn't feel like going on many adventures anymore. But they'd still like to visit the lion cub.

What could she be dreaming?

Piloten flyr og flyr. Til verdens ende, og videre helt til stjernene. Ingen pilot har klart dette før ham.

Når drømmen er over, er alle veldig trøtte og vil ikke oppleve så mye mer.

Men løveungen vil de likevel hilse på. Hva drømmer han om?

The lion cub is homesick and wants to go back to the warm, cozy bed.
And so do the others.

And thus begins ...

Løveungen har hjemlengsel og vil tilbake til den varme, deilige senga si.
Det vil de andre også.

Og da begynner ...

... Lulu's
most beautiful dream.

... Lulus
aller fineste drøm.

Foto: Ingrid Hagenreich

Cornelia Haas was born near Augsburg, Germany, in 1972. After completing her apprenticeship as a sign and light advertising manufacturer, she studied design at the Münster University of Applied Sciences and graduated with a degree in design. Since 2001 she has been illustrating childrens' and adolescents' books, since 2013 she has been teaching acrylic and digital painting at the Münster University of Applied Sciences.

Cornelia Haas ble født i nærheten av Augsburg (Tyskland) i 1972. Hun studerte design ved Høgskolen i Münster og avsluttet studiene med diplom. Siden 2001 har hun illustrert barne- og ungdomsbøker. Siden 2013 har hun undervist i akryl- og digitalt maleri ved Høgskolen i Münster.

www.cornelia-haas.de

Do you like drawing?

Here are the pictures from the story to color in:

www.sefa-bilingual.com/coloring

Enjoy!

Dear Reader,

Thanks for choosing my book! If you (and most of all, your child) liked it, please spread the word via a Facebook-Like or an email to your friends:

www.sefa-bilingual.com/like

I would also be happy to get a comment or a review. Likes and comments are great „Tender Loving Care" for authors, thanks so much!

If there is no audiobook version in your language yet, please be patient! We are working on making all the languages available as audiobooks. You can check the „Language Wizard" for the latest updates:

www.sefa-bilingual.com/languages

Now let me briefly introduce myself: I was born in Stuttgart in 1960, together with my twin brother Herbert (who also became a writer). I studied French literature and a couple of languages in Paris, then medicine in Lübeck. However, my career as a doctor was brief because I soon discovered books: medical books at first, for which I was an editor and a publisher, and later non-fiction and children's books.

I live with my wife Kirsten in Lübeck in the very north of Germany; together we have three (now grown) children, a dog, two cats, and a little publishing house: Sefa Press.

If you want to know more about me, you are welcome to visit my website: **www.ulrichrenz.de**

Best regards,

Ulrich Renz

Lulu also recommends:

Sleep Tight, Little Wolf

For ages 2 and up

with online audio and video

Tim can't fall asleep. His little wolf is missing! Perhaps he forgot him outside?
Tim heads out all alone into the night – and unexpectedly encounters some friends …

Available in your languages?

► Check out with our „Language Wizard":

www.sefa-bilingual.com/languages

The Wild Swans

Based on a fairy tale by
Hans Christian Andersen

Recommended age: 4-5
and up

with online audio and
video

„The Wild Swans" by Hans Christian Andersen is, with good reason, one of the world's most popular fairy tales. In its timeless form it addresses the issues out of which human dramas are made: fear, bravery, love, betrayal, separation and reunion.

Available in your languages?

► Check out with our „Language Wizard":

www.sefa-bilingual.com/languages

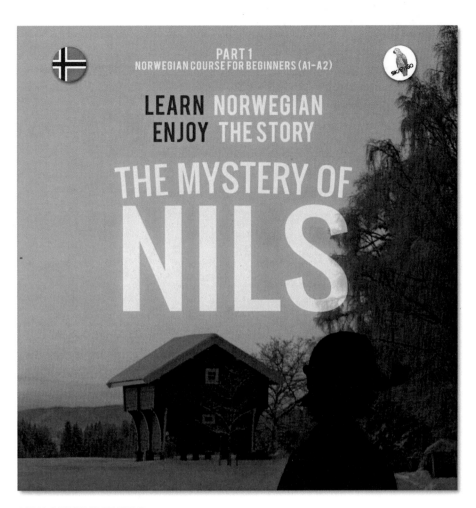

ISBN **9783945174005**

Learn Norwegian with a fascinating story!

Would you like to read a fun story while getting serious instruction in grammar and vocabulary?

Then you should have a look at "The Mystery of Nils" by Skapago Publishing. You can learn Norwegian with a coherent story that starts very simply, yet gets more and more advanced as the story progresses. Would you like to know how the story ends? If so…..you will just have to learn Norwegian!

For more information and a free preview see

www.skapago.eu

More of me ...

Bo & Friends

► Children's detective series in three volumes. Reading age: 9+

► German Edition: „Motte & Co" ► www.motte-und-co.de

► Download the series' first volume, „Bo and the Blackmailers" for free!

www.bo-and-friends.com/free

IT: Paul Bödeker, Freiburg, Germany

ISBN: 9783739962634

Version: 20190101

www.sefa-bilingual.com